© Emma Brown 2023

Published by The Poetry House.

All rights reserved. No part of this publication may be reproduced, stored in a retrieval system, or transmitted in any form or by any means, electronic, mechanical, photocopying, recording or otherwise, without prior permission of the author.

ISBN Paperback: 978-1-7385841-2-3
ISBN eBook: 978-1-7385841-3-0

Table of Contents

Introduction 4

1. Invictus (Unconquered) 1
2. Love is Patient, Love is Kind 2
3. To Strive, to Seek, to Find, and not to Yield 3
4. The Light of a Candle 6
5. If- 7
6. These I can Promise 9
7. A Psalm of Life 10
8. Courage 12
9. Pick More Daisies 13
10. Take Time (To dream) 15
11. Hope 17
12. Don't Quit 18
13. May the Road Rise up to Meet You 19
14. This is Faith 20
15. Daffodils 21
16. The Road Not Taken (Made all the difference) 22
17. The Owl and the Pussy-Cat 23
18. Tyger Tyger, Burning Bright 25
19. The Lake Isle of Innisfree 26
20. Jabberwocky 27
21. Shall I Compare Thee to a Summer's Day? 28
22. The Wild Swans at Coole 29
23. She Walks in Beauty 30
24. Success (Live well, laugh often, and love much) 31

25.	The Old Pond	32
26.	See it Through	33
27.	Never Surrender	34
28.	Jerusalem (And did those feet in ancient time)	35
29.	Desiderata (Go placidly amid the noise)	36
30.	Inspirational Quotes	38
31.	Journaling Prompts	40
32.	Positive Affirmations to Start My Day	42

Introduction

Nurturing our mental health and well-being is more important than ever and I hope this short book, which collates inspirational poems, positive affirmations, and journaling prompts, helps restore your mental grit, courage, and resilience.

Carpe Diem!
Seize the Day!

Emma Brown

1. Invictus (Unconquered)

Out of the night that covers me,
    Black as the pit from pole to pole,
I thank whatever gods may be
    For my unconquerable soul.

In the fell clutch of circumstance
    I have not winced nor cried aloud.
Under the bludgeonings of chance
    My head is bloody, but unbowed.

Beyond this place of wrath and tears
    Looms but the Horror of the shade,
And yet the menace of the years
    Finds and shall find me unafraid.

It matters not how strait the gate,
    How charged with punishments the scroll,
I am the master of my fate,
    I am the captain of my soul.

William Ernest Henley
1888

2. Love is Patient, Love is Kind

Love is patient, love is kind.
It does not envy, it does not boast,
it is not proud.
It does not dishonour others,
it is not self-seeking,
it is not easily angered,
and it keeps no record of wrongs.

Love does not delight in evil
but rejoices with the truth.
It always protects,
always trusts,
always hopes,
and always perseveres.

Love never fails.

1 Corinthians 13

3. To Strive, to Seek, to Find, and not to Yield

It little profits that an idle king,
By this still hearth, among these barren crags,
Match'd with an aged wife, I mete and dole
Unequal laws unto a savage race,
That hoard, and sleep, and feed, and know not me.

I cannot rest from travel: I will drink
Life to the lees: All times I have enjoy'd
Greatly, have suffer'd greatly, both with those
That loved me, and alone, on shore, and when
Thro' scudding drifts the rainy Hyades
Vext the dim sea: I am become a name;

For always roaming with a hungry heart
Much have I seen and known; cities of men
And manners, climates, councils, governments,
Myself not least, but honour'd of them all;
And drunk delight of battle with my peers,
Far on the ringing plains of windy Troy.

I am a part of all that I have met;
Yet all experience is an arch wherethro'
Gleams that untravell'd world whose margin fades
For ever and forever when I move.

How dull it is to pause, to make an end,
To rust unburnish'd, not to shine in use!
As tho' to breathe were life! Life piled on life
Were all too little, and of one to me
Little remains: but every hour is saved

From that eternal silence, something more,
A bringer of new things; and vile it were
For some three suns to store and hoard myself,
And this gray spirit yearning in desire
To follow knowledge like a sinking star,
Beyond the utmost bound of human thought.

  This is my son, mine own Telemachus,
To whom I leave the sceptre and the isle,—
Well-loved of me, discerning to fulfil
This labour, by slow prudence to make mild
A rugged people, and thro' soft degrees
Subdue them to the useful and the good.

Most blameless is he, centred in the sphere
Of common duties, decent not to fail
In offices of tenderness, and pay
Meet adoration to my household gods,
When I am gone. He works his work, I mine.

  There lies the port; the vessel puffs her sail:
There gloom the dark, broad seas. My mariners,
Souls that have toil'd, and wrought,
and thought with me—
That ever with a frolic welcome took
The thunder and the sunshine, and opposed
Free hearts, free foreheads—you and I are old;
Old age hath yet his honour and his toil;
Death closes all: but something ere the end,
Some work of noble note, may yet be done,
Not unbecoming men that strove with Gods.

Emma Brown

The lights begin to twinkle from the rocks:
The long day wanes: the slow moon climbs: the deep
Moans round with many voices. Come, my friends,
'T is not too late to seek a newer world.

Push off, and sitting well in order smite
The sounding furrows; for my purpose holds
To sail beyond the sunset, and the baths
Of all the western stars, until I die.

It may be that the gulfs will wash us down:
It may be we shall touch the Happy Isles,
And see the great Achilles, whom we knew.

Tho' much is taken, much abides; and tho'
We are not now that strength which in old days
Moved earth and heaven, that which we are, we are;
One equal temper of heroic hearts,
Made weak by time and fate, but strong in will
To strive, to seek, to find, and not to yield.

Ulysses, Alfred, Lord Tennyson
1842

4. The Light of a Candle

The light of a candle
Is transferred to another candle —
spring twilight.

Yosa Buson
(Japanese Haiku)

5.   If-

If you can keep your head when all about you
    Are losing theirs and blaming it on you,
If you can trust yourself when all men doubt you,
    But make allowance for their doubting too;
If you can wait and not be tired by waiting,
    Or being lied about, don't deal in lies,
Or being hated, don't give way to hating,
    And yet don't look too good, nor talk too wise:

If you can dream—and not make dreams your master;
    If you can think—and not make thoughts your aim;
If you can meet with Triumph and Disaster
    And treat those two impostors just the same;
If you can bear to hear the truth you've spoken
    Twisted by knaves to make a trap for fools,
Or watch the things you gave your life to, broken,
    And stoop and build 'em up with worn-out tools:

If you can make one heap of all your winnings
    And risk it on one turn of pitch-and-toss,
And lose, and start again at your beginnings
    And never breathe a word about your loss;
If you can force your heart and nerve and sinew
    To serve your turn long after they are gone,
And so hold on when there is nothing in you
    Except the Will which says to them: 'Hold on!'

If you can talk with crowds and keep your virtue,
    Or walk with Kings—nor lose the common touch,
If neither foes nor loving friends can hurt you,
    If all men count with you, but none too much;

If you can fill the unforgiving minute
    With sixty seconds' worth of distance run,
Yours is the Earth and everything that's in it,
    And—which is more
    —you'll be a Man, my son!

Rudyard Kipling
1910

Emma Brown

6. These I can Promise

I cannot promise you a life of sunshine;
I cannot promise riches, wealth or gold;
I cannot promise you an easy pathway
that leads away from change or growing old.

But I can promise all my heart's devotion;
a smile to chase away your tears of sorrow;
a love that's ever true and ever growing;
and a hand to hold in yours
through each tomorrow.

Anon

7. A Psalm of Life

What The Heart Of The Young Man Said To The Psalmist.

Tell me not, in mournful numbers,
   Life is but an empty dream!
For the soul is dead that slumbers,
   And things are not what they seem.

Life is real! Life is earnest!
   And the grave is not its goal;
Dust thou art, to dust returnest,
   Was not spoken of the soul.

Not enjoyment, and not sorrow,
   Is our destined end or way;
But to act, that each to-morrow
   Find us farther than to-day.

Art is long, and Time is fleeting,
   And our hearts, though stout and brave,
Still, like muffled drums, are beating
   Funeral marches to the grave.

In the world's broad field of battle,
   In the bivouac of Life,
Be not like dumb, driven cattle!
   Be a hero in the strife!

Trust no Future, howe'er pleasant!
   Let the dead Past bury its dead!
Act,— act in the living Present!
   Heart within, and God o'erhead!

Emma Brown

Lives of great men all remind us
   We can make our lives sublime,
And, departing, leave behind us
   Footprints on the sands of time;

Footprints, that perhaps another,
   Sailing o'er life's solemn main,
A forlorn and shipwrecked brother,
   Seeing, shall take heart again.

Let us, then, be up and doing,
   With a heart for any fate;
Still achieving, still pursuing,
   Learn to labor and to wait.

Henry Wadsworth Longfellow
1838

8. Courage

Courage isn't a brilliant dash,
A daring deed in a moment's flash;
It isn't an instantaneous thing
Born of despair with a sudden spring
It isn't a creature of flickered hope
Or the final tug at a slipping rope;
But it's something deep in the soul of man
That is working always to serve some plan.

Courage isn't the last resort
In the work of life or the game of sport;
It isn't a thing that a man can call
At some future time when he's apt to fall;
If he hasn't it now, he will have it not
When the strain is great and the pace is hot.
For who would strive for a distant goal
Must always have courage within his soul.

Courage isn't a dazzling light
That flashes and passes away from sight;
It's a slow, unwavering, ingrained trait
With the patience to work and the strength to wait.
It's part of a man when his skies are blue,
It's part of him when he has work to do.
The brave man never is freed of it.
He has it when there is no need of it.

Courage was never designed for show;
It isn't a thing that can come and go;
It's written in victory and defeat
And every trial a man may meet.
It's part of his hours, his days and his years,
Back of his smiles and behind his tears.
Courage is more than a daring deed:
It's the breath of life and a strong man's creed.

Edgar Albert Guest

Emma Brown

9. Pick More Daisies

If I had my life to live over;
I'd dare to make more mistakes next time.
I'd relax. I would limber up.
I would be sillier than I have been this trip.
I would take fewer things seriously.
I would take more chances.
I would take more trips.
I would climb more mountains and swim more rivers.
I would eat more ice cream and less beans.

I would perhaps have more actual troubles but
I'd have fewer imaginary ones.

You see, I'm one of those people who live sensibly
and sanely hour after hour, day after day.

Oh, I've had my moments
and if I had it to do over again,
I'd have more of them.
In fact, I'd try to have nothing else.
Just moments.

One after another,
instead of living so many years
ahead of each day.

I've been one of those people
who never go anywhere without a thermometer,
a hot water bottle, a raincoat and a parachute.

If I had my life to live over,
I would start barefoot earlier in the spring
and stay that way later in the fall.

If I had it to do again,
I would travel lighter next time.
I would go to more dances.
I would ride more merry-go-rounds.
I would pick more daisies.

Attributed to Nadine Stair
(age 85)

10. Take Time (To dream)

Take time to dream,
it is hitching your soul to the stars.

Take time to work,
it is the price of success.

Take time to think,
it is the source of power.

Take time to play,
it is the secret of perpetual youth.

Take time to read,
it is the foundation of knowledge.

Take time for worship,
it is the highway of reverence
and washes the dust of the earth from your eyes.

Take time to be friendly,
it is the road to happiness.

Take time to help and enjoy friends,
it is the source of happiness.

Take time to love and be loved,
it is the sacrament of life.

Take time to laugh,
it is the music of the soul.

Take time for beauty,
it is everywhere in nature.

Take time to look around,
it is too short a day to be selfish.

Take time for health,
it is the true treasure of life.

Anon

Emma Brown

11. Hope

Hope is the thing with feathers
That perches in the soul,
And sings the tune without the words,
And never stops at all,

And sweetest in the gale is heard;
And sore must be the storm
That could abash the little bird
That kept so many warm.

I've heard it in the chillest land,
And on the strangest Sea;
Yet, never, in extremity,
It asked a crumb of me.

Emily Dickinson
1891

12. Don't Quit

When things go wrong,
as they sometimes will,
When the road you're trudging seems all uphill,
When the funds are low but the debts are high,
And you want to smile but you have to sigh,
When care is pressing you down a bit,
Rest if you must, but don't you quit.

Life is strange with its twists and turns,
As every one of us sometimes learns,
And many failures turn about
When we might have won had we stuck it out.
Don't give up though the pace seems slow –
You may succeed with another blow.

Success is failure turned inside out –
The silver tint of the clouds of doubt,
You can never tell how close you are,
It may be near when it seems so far;
So stick to the fight when you're hardest hit –
It's when things seem worst
that you must not quit.

Edgar A. Guest

Emma Brown

13.   May the Road Rise up to Meet You

May the road rise up to meet you.
May the wind be always at your back.
May the sun shine warm upon your face;
the rains fall soft upon your fields
and until we meet again,
may God hold you in the palm of His hand.

Traditional Gaelic Blessing

14. This is Faith

To walk where there is no path
To breathe where there is no air
To see where there is no light
- This is Faith.

To cry out in the silence,
The silence of the night,
And hearing no echo believe
And believe again and again
- This is Faith.

To hold pebbles and see jewels
To raise sticks and see forests
To smile with weeping eyes
- This is Faith.

To say: "God, I believe" when others deny,
"I hear" when there is no answer,
"I see" though naught is seen
- This is Faith.

And the fierce love in the heart,
The savage love that cries
Hidden Thou art yet there!
Veil Thy face and mute Thy tongue
Yet I see and hear Thee, Love,
Beat me down to the bare earth,
Yet I rise and love Thee, Love!
This is Faith.

Ruhiyyih (Mary Maxwell) Khanum
1954

15. Daffodils

I wandered lonely as a cloud
That floats on high o'er vales and hills,
When all at once I saw a crowd,
A host, of golden daffodils;
Beside the lake, beneath the trees,
Fluttering and dancing in the breeze.

Continuous as the stars that shine
And twinkle on the milky way,
They stretched in never-ending line
Along the margin of a bay:
Ten thousand saw I at a glance,
Tossing their heads in sprightly dance.

The waves beside them danced;
but they Out-did the sparkling waves in glee:
A poet could not but be gay,
In such a jocund company:
I gazed—and gazed—but little thought
What wealth the show to me had brought:

For oft, when on my couch I lie
In vacant or in pensive mood,
They flash upon that inward eye
Which is the bliss of solitude;
And then my heart with pleasure fills,
And dances with the daffodils.

William Wordsworth
1807

16. The Road Not Taken (Made all the difference)

Two roads diverged in a yellow wood,
And sorry I could not travel both
And be one traveller, long I stood
And looked down one as far as I could
To where it bent in the undergrowth;

Then took the other, as just as fair,
And having perhaps the better claim,
Because it was grassy and wanted wear;
Though as for that the passing there
Had worn them really about the same,

And both that morning equally lay
In leaves no step had trodden black.
Oh, I kept the first for another day!
Yet knowing how way leads on to way,
I doubted if I should ever come back.

I shall be telling this with a sigh
Somewhere ages and ages hence:
Two roads diverged in a wood, and I—
I took the one less travelled by,
And that has made all the difference.

Robert Frost
1915

17. The Owl and the Pussy-Cat

The Owl and the Pussy-cat went to sea
  In a beautiful pea-green boat,
They took some honey,
  and plenty of money,
Wrapped up in a five-pound note.

The Owl looked up to the stars above,
  And sang to a small guitar,
"O lovely Pussy!
  O Pussy, my love,
What a beautiful Pussy you are,
  You are, You are!
What a beautiful Pussy you are!"

Pussy said to the Owl,
  "You elegant fowl!
How charmingly sweet you sing!
  O let us be married!
  too long we have tarried:
But what shall we do for a ring?"

They sailed away, for a year and a day,
  To the land where the Bong-Tree grows
And there in a wood a Piggy-wig stood
  With a ring at the end of his nose,
His nose, His nose,
  With a ring at the end of his nose.

"Dear Pig, are you willing to sell
  for one shilling Your ring?"
Said the Piggy, "I will."
  So they took it away,
  and were married next day
By the Turkey who lives on the hill.

They dined on mince, and slices of quince,
   Which they ate with a runcible spoon;
And hand in hand, on the edge of the sand,
   They danced by the light of the moon,
   The moon, The moon,
They danced by the light of the moon.

Edward Lear
1871

Emma Brown

18.   Tyger Tyger, Burning Bright

Tyger Tyger, burning bright,
In the forests of the night;
What immortal hand or eye,
Could frame thy fearful symmetry?

In what distant deeps or skies.
Burnt the fire of thine eyes?
On what wings dare he aspire?
What the hand, dare seize the fire?

And what shoulder, and what art,
Could twist the sinews of thy heart?
And when thy heart began to beat.
What dread hand? And what dread feet?

What the hammer? what the chain,
In what furnace was thy brain?
What the anvil? what dread grasp.
Dare its deadly terrors clasp?

When the stars threw down their spears
And water'd heaven with their tears:
Did he smile his work to see?
Did he who made the Lamb make thee?

Tyger Tyger burning bright,
In the forests of the night:
What immortal hand or eye,
Dare frame thy fearful symmetry?

William Blake
1794

19. The Lake Isle of Innisfree

I will arise and go now,
and go to Innisfree,
And a small cabin build there,
of clay and wattles made;
Nine bean-rows will I have there,
a hive for the honey-bee,
And live alone in the bee-loud glade.

And I shall have some peace there,
for peace comes dropping slow,
Dropping from the veils of the morning
to where the cricket sings;
There midnight's all a glimmer,
and noon a purple glow,
And evening full of the linnet's wings.

I will arise and go now,
for always night and day
I hear lake water lapping
with low sounds by the shore;
While I stand on the roadway,
or on the pavements grey,
I hear it in the deep heart's core.

William Butler Yeats
1890

20. Jabberwocky

'Twas as brillig, and the slithy toves
    Did gyre and gimble in the wabe:
All mimsy were the borogoves,
    And the mome raths outgrabe.

"Beware the Jabberwock, my son!
    The jaws that bite, the claws that catch!
Beware the Jubjub bird, and shun
    The frumious Bandersnatch!"

He took his vorpal sword in hand;
    Long time the manxome foe he
sought— So rested he by the Tumtum tree
    And stood awhile in thought.

And, as in uffish thought he stood,
    The Jabberwock, with eyes of flame,
Came whiffling through the tulgey wood,
    And burbled as it came!

One, two! One, two! And through and through
    The vorpal blade went snicker-snack!
He left it dead, and with its head
    He went galumphing back.

"And hast thou slain the Jabberwock?
    Come to my arms, my beamish boy!
O frabjous day! Callooh! Callay!"
    He chortled in his joy.

'Twas brillig, and the slithy toves
    Did gyre and gimble in the wabe:
All mimsy were the borogoves,
    And the mome raths outgrabe.

Lewis Carroll
1871

21.   Shall I Compare Thee to a Summer's Day?

Shall I compare thee to a summer's day?
Thou art more lovely and more temperate:
Rough winds do shake the darling buds of May,
And summer's lease hath all too short a date;

Sometime too hot the eye of heaven shines,
And often is his gold complexion dimm'd;
And every fair from fair sometime declines,
By chance or nature's changing course untrimm'd;

But thy eternal summer shall not fade,
Nor lose possession of that fair thou ow'st;
Nor shall death brag thou wander'st in his shade,
When in eternal lines to time thou grow'st:

So long as men can breathe or eyes can see,
So long lives this, and this gives life to thee.

Sonnet 18
William Shakespeare
1609

Emma Brown

22.   The Wild Swans at Coole

The trees are in their autumn beauty,
The woodland paths are dry,
Under the October twilight
the water Mirrors a still sky;
Upon the brimming water among the stones
Are nine-and-fifty swans.

The nineteenth autumn has come upon me
Since I first made my count;
I saw, before I had well finished,
All suddenly mount
And scatter wheeling in great broken rings
Upon their clamorous wings.

I have looked upon those brilliant creatures,
And now my heart is sore.
All's changed since I, hearing at twilight,
The first time on this shore,
The bell-beat of their wings above my head,
Trod with a lighter tread.

Unwearied still, lover by lover,
They paddle in the cold
Companionable streams or climb the air;
Their hearts have not grown old;
Passion or conquest, wander where they will,
Attend upon them still.

But now they drift on the still water,
Mysterious, beautiful;
Among what rushes will they build,
By what lake's edge or pool
Delight men's eyes when I awake some day
To find they have flown away?

William Butler Yeats, 1917

23. She Walks in Beauty

She walks in beauty, like the night
Of cloudless climes and starry skies;
And all that's best of dark and bright
Meet in her aspect and her eyes;
Thus mellowed to that tender light
Which heaven to gaudy day denies.

One shade the more, one ray the less,
Had half impaired the nameless grace
Which waves in every raven tress,
Or softly lightens o'er her face;
Where thoughts serenely sweet express,
How pure, how dear their dwelling-place.

And on that cheek, and o'er that brow,
So soft, so calm, yet eloquent,
The smiles that win, the tints that glow,
But tell of days in goodness spent,
A mind at peace with all below,
A heart whose love is innocent!

Lord Byron (George Gordon)
1814

Emma Brown

24. Success (Live well, laugh often, and love much)

He achieved success who has lived well,
laughed often, and loved much;
Who has enjoyed the trust of pure women,
the respect of intelligent men,
and the love of little children;
Who has filled his niche and accomplished his task;
Who has never lacked appreciation of Earth's beauty,
or failed to express it;
Who has left the world better than he found it,
Whether an improved poppy, a perfect poem,
or a rescued soul;
Who has always looked for the best in others,
and given them the best he had;
Whose life was an inspiration;
Whose memory a benediction.

— Success

Bessie Anderson Stanley
1904

25. The Old Pond

An old silent pond
A frog jumps into the pond
— Splash!
Silence again.

Matsuo Bashō
(Japanese Haiku)

26.   See it Through

When you're up against a trouble,
  Meet it squarely, face to face;
Lift your chin and set your shoulders,
  Plant your feet and take a brace.
When it's vain to try to dodge it,
  Do the best that you can do;
You may fail, but you may conquer,
  See it through!

Black may be the clouds about you
  And your future may seem grim,
But don't let your nerve desert you;
  Keep yourself in fighting trim.
If the worst is bound to happen,
  Spite of all that you can do,
Running from it will not save you,
  See it through!

Even hope may seem but futile,
  When with troubles you're beset,
But remember you are facing
  Just what other men have met.
You may fail, but fall still fighting;
  Don't give up, whate'er you do;
Eyes front, head high to the finish.
  See it through!

Edgar Albert Guest
1917

27. Never Surrender

Winston Churchill delivered the
"We Shall Fight on the Beaches" speech in 1940,
showing the strength of the human spirit.

Emma Brown

28. Jerusalem (And did those feet in ancient time)

And did those feet in ancient time
  Walk upon England's mountains green:
And was the holy Lamb of God,
  On England's pleasant pastures seen!

And did the Countenance Divine,
  Shine forth upon our clouded hills?
And was Jerusalem builded here,
  Among these dark Satanic Mills?

Bring me my Bow of burning gold:
  Bring me my arrows of desire:
Bring me my Spear: O clouds unfold!
  Bring me my Chariot of fire!

I will not ccase from Mental Fight,
  Nor shall my sword sleep in my hand:
Till we have built Jerusalem,
  In England's green and pleasant Land.

William Blake
1804

29. Desiderata (Go placidly amid the noise)

Go placidly amid the noise and the haste,
   and remember what peace there may be in silence.
As far as possible, without surrender,
   be on good terms with all persons.

Speak your truth quietly and clearly;
   and listen to others,
Even to the dull and the ignorant;
   they too have their story.

Avoid loud and aggressive persons;
   they are vexatious to the spirit.
If you compare yourself with others,
   you may become vain or bitter,
For always there will be greater
   and lesser persons than yourself.

Enjoy your achievements
   as well as your plans.
Keep interested in your own career,
   however humble;
It is a real possession
   in the changing fortunes of time.

Exercise caution in your business affairs,
   for the world is full of trickery.
But let this not blind you
   to what virtue there is;
Many persons strive for high ideals,
   and everywhere life is full of heroism.

Be yourself.
   Especially do not feign affection.
Neither be cynical about love;
   for in the face of all aridity and disenchantment,
   it is as perennial as the grass.

Emma Brown

Take kindly the counsel of the years,
  gracefully surrendering the things of youth.

Nurture strength of spirit
  to shield you in sudden misfortune.
But do not distress yourself with dark imaginings.
  Many fears are born of fatigue and loneliness.

Beyond a wholesome discipline,
  be gentle with yourself.
You are a child of the universe
  no less than the trees and the stars;
You have a right to be here.

And whether or not it is clear to you,
  no doubt the universe is unfolding as it should.
Therefore be at peace with God,
  whatever you conceive Him to be.

And whatever your labors and aspirations,
  in the noisy confusion of life,
Keep peace in your soul.

With all its sham, drudgery and broken dreams,
it is still a beautiful world.

Be cheerful. Strive to be happy.

Max Ehrmann
1927

30. Inspirational Quotes

"To live is the rarest thing in the world.
Most people just exist."
- Oscar Wilde

"Be yourself; everyone else is already taken."
- Oscar Wilde

"Wherever you go, go with all your heart."
- Confucius

"Magic is believing in yourself,
if you can do that, you can make anything happen."
- Johann Wolfgang von Goethe

"The secret of change is to focus all of your energy,
not on fighting the old, but on building the new."
- Socrates

"We are what we repeatedly do.
Excellence, then, is not an act, but a habit."
- Aristotle

"No man is free who is not master of himself."
- Epictetus

"It is never too late to be what you might have been."
- George Eliot

"Do small things with great love."
- Mother Teresa

"No act of kindness, no matter how small, is ever wasted."
- Aesop

"It is better to travel well than to arrive."
- *Buddha*

"Look deep into nature,
and then you will understand everything better."
- *Albert Einstein*

"Our greatest glory is not in never falling,
but in rising every time we fall"
- *Confucius*

"In seeking happiness for others,
you will find it in yourself."
- *Anon*

31. Journaling Prompts

For centuries, people have kept diaries as their trusted friends and as a safe harbour to reflect on daily experiences, relationships, and their peace of mind.

Consider creating a writing routine and get creative.

Start with a poem or reflection;

Protect your privacy; and

Date every entry.

Write quickly, and naturally. Let your thoughts and feelings flow onto the paper.

"For it is only with the heart that one can see well."
- *Le Petit Prince, The Little Prince,*
  (Antoine de Saint-Exupéry)

Emma Brown

Journal prompts:

Write down what brings you joy.

Describe a place where you felt happiest.

Write a letter to someone you have always wanted to thank but have never had the chance to do so.

Write down what happened today.

Write down what went well today.

Write down what you learnt today.

And write down how you will you make tomorrow even better.

32. Positive Affirmations to Start My Day

Take a few minutes at the start of each day to say a few of these life-changing positive affirmations so that you can have a really great day.

Happiness is a choice, and I choose to be happy.
I am successful. I am confident. I am powerful. I am strong.

I am getting stronger every day.
I am having a positive impact on the people
I come into contact with.
I am focused.
I inspire people through my work.
And my soul radiates from the inside and
warms the souls of others.

Today is a phenomenal day.
I am independent and self-sufficient.
I keep track of things.
I am in charge of my finances, plan for my future, and manage what I spend.
I am grateful for food on my table, a roof over my head, and for everything I have in my life.

Today is a wonderful day.
My life has meaning.
I am intelligent and focused.
I am strong and getting stronger every day.
I am relaxed; I am prepared; and I am strong.

I believe in me.
I respect myself.
I love myself deeply and fully.
My skin is healthy, glowing, and deeply nourished.
My life is filled with abundance and all that is good.

Today is filled with possibility.
I have strengths, abilities, and talent.
And am not defined by my past mistakes.
I have set personal goals for today and for the life I desire.
I believe in myself and I look forward to today.

I am a beautiful human being.
I breathe. I live. And I choose to be happy.

My life is filled with promise and purpose.
I am thankful.
I am prepared; and
I am confident about today.
I will create a safe place for myself today and everyday.

I am ready to start my day.
I am focused, centred, and at peace.
I will succeed by enjoying this day fully.
I will be kind to myself and compliment others.
And everything will be okay!

www.ingramcontent.com/pod-product-compliance
Lightning Source LLC
Chambersburg PA
CBHW070339120526
44590CB00017B/2954